A Pathway

Poems by
Margaret O. Daramola

A Pathway Through Survival

ISBN: 978-3-9525377-0-1

Contact Margaret Daramola on her website

www.maggiedaramola.com

A Pathway Through Survival

Table of Contents

To myself,
the person I once was
and the one I then became.

To you,
the person you now are
and the one you will soon become.

To God,
for carrying me through.

I have memories of that day
as if it were yesterday.
The day two wings placed me on a path
I knew nothing about.
Their wings–so light yet so heavy,
so bright, that their gleam overwhelmed my sight.
It was like a dream to me.
I remember as they graciously led me
towards my first steps,
the ease I felt, the confidence I had.
Although this path was foreign to me,
I trusted the wings who had placed me there.

Thirst

Autumn Leaves

Mother gave birth to me in the fall
in the midst of grieving trees and withering leaves.
Winter came home right after
accompanied by winds of solitude.
My earliest memories revolved around cold weather
yet I remember meeting with summer
before ever blowing my first candle.
I saw these same trees shimmer in full bloom.
I saw their branches clothed in vivid green.

Early on,
I learned not to shed a tear when autumn leaves
for I know that summer comes home through the shiver.

Tom & Jerry

I grew up watching Tom and Jerry.
As I sat the core of the living room
eye to eye with a TV that I saw
but couldn't see me,
I watched Tom chase Jerry
and Jerry hide from Tom.
They would often switch roles,
run after each other, hide from each other,
only to come right back
and meet each other.
I knew Tom would always have his way
and Jerry would always runaway-
without ever fully going away.

At such a young age
I sat confused and wondered,
"What is it about Tom
that keeps Jerry coming back
again and again,
hoping that this time she would catch him
finally have her way
and convince him to stay?"

I never really understood Jerry.

Perhaps they were so used to the harm
they caused each other
that they learned to embrace it,

they learn to accept it,
no matter how much it confused the people
who were there watching TV.

Perhaps somewhere in their beginnings,
they lived peacefully.
Perhaps the Tom that I saw
wasn't the one that she could see.
Perhaps that is why it would take years
for me to understand Jerry.

I grew up watching Tom and Jerry
yet I didn't have the luxury of changing channels
or switching off the TV.
So I grew up thinking that Tom and Jerry
was the only cartoon there for me.

Childhood Lullabies

When I hear the intro,
I hear the sound of a past decade,
one that awakens memories at every beat.
It speaks to me in a language foreign to everyone else.
It knows me in ways that only a few ever will.

These lullabies take me back to a well-known place.
A place I would recognize even with closed eyes.
As the verse plays, my mind wanders
whilst I smile at the smell of freshly cooked kebab.
Reminiscing the mothers in wrappers
who carried groceries and told stories,
at the teens in baggies
holding Mp3's of J-lo and Fat Joe,
balling with dreams of one day making it to the NBA.

When the chorus comes on
I see people who learned to survive
with the little they had.
I see kids who were happy and smiled on a daily
I see myself, oblivious to the reality
that swept the world around me.
Because in innocence, the chaos is colorless.

My heart ponders
as I listen to the outro.
It reminds me to hold dear
the seeds that were planted within me.

The Things We Had in Common

She was strong
A woman of great endurance
When the storm would reach its peak
And the waves would search for peace
She was patient
When hardship knocked on the door
And failure walked in once more
She was resilient

From her
I gained great tolerance
For the things that tried to break me
Slowly and quietly
Just like her
I felt pain run through my veins
Yet unlike her
I refused to let it overstay

Daddy's Girl

He raised me to be fearless.
He taught me that some people will only love me
to the extent of their capacity.
Although it might make sense in their ears,
they will speak to me with vowels
I will not comprehend.
Soaked in a bathtub of guilt
I will wonder why they are not fluent in my language.
Only to realize that
some people grew up in a different part of the world,
some, can only speak the language
that was first taught to them.

With the lessons Daddy taught me,
I learned to keep my tears
when promises turned to ashes
before ever becoming flame.
I learned that I have not myself to blame.

Temporary Shelters

I know of men with holes
who carry wounds
and place them within wombs.
They roam about,
searching for security
within a woman's body.
Because the only place
they've ever felt at home
was in their mother's body.
In longing for that same feeling,
they search and search and search.

These men, carry wounds
and place them within wombs.
Addicted to the warmth,
they hope to find shelter within a stranger,
only to come out feeling colder and emptier.

The void is not gone.
The bleeding is still on.
*Temporary shelters
do not keep you warm forever.*

Margaret O. Daramola

They say men don't cry
and perhaps that is why
I never saw teardrops
fall down my father's eye.

Men don't cry
until their bones grow weary
of not being able to.

With a mask of indifference,
they hide the very parts of themselves
designed to be seen, felt and comforted.

They "man up"
and allow the pain to build up,
yet die on the inside.
Because someone once told them,
A man must never show emotion.

Men don't cry–in tears.
They cry–in anger.

Outcast

How does one survive in the desert
When rain forgets to kiss the drought?

She was sent into the unknown
Alone in the wilderness of 'Sheba
She wandered through the Sahara
Holding on to nothing but an empty jar
Aimlessly sitting on dry soil
With only her cry to lift up to the Most High
Hope soon became an old friend
While despair was there to replace it
It was in her greatest anguish that
He showed up to her.
Quenched her thirst as he filled her cup
Wrapping his comfort around her shoulders
He whispered
You are heard my daughter.

Margaret O. Daramola

Even in the wilderness,
He hears your voice.

Sisters of Different Generations

On days where I struggle to believe
that there is beauty in the process,
I remember Hagar
who fought to find reason
in a season of weeping and doubting
before ever obtaining the strength
to unravel her blessing.

She is like me and I am as her.

Hagar brings back memories
of days my feet felt too weak to stand tall.
She evokes souvenirs of a heartache
that seemed too severe to be cured.
But Hagar gave birth to Ishmael.
A nation raised after him.
A miracle on his own.
If Hagar was able to breakthrough
then who am I not to?

For she is like me and I am as her.
Sisters of different generations.

Desert Spoon

In your company,
my branch began to weaken,
my petals began to run dry.
For so long, I longed to be refilled.

I am the flower you failed to water.
I should have known better,
not to plant myself alongside a fountain
that does not run consistently.
I am the flower you failed to water.

I am also
the flower that did not die in aridity.
I am that same flower
that learned to unfold her petals in a dry season.

Hunger

Margaret O. Daramola

We walked side by side
You promised to hold me down
Yet there I was
Falling apart

I should have known then
That it was time
To walk away

Drifting Away

One day you hold them tight
they seem so close to you
your palms match theirs
as perfectly as the Jupiter symphony.
Then suddenly
they begin to drift away
and before you know it
or have time to realize it
they are now faraway.
Too far to remember.
Too far to see or understand.
When you finally cross their path again
their eyes are no longer the same.
They scream void.
When you look into the depth of their pupils
all you see is emptiness.
Unfamiliar. Unaware. Unknown.
How easily they forget.
How easily they disappear.
They waft from best friends to strangers,
from lovers to haters,
from family to enemy.

Perhaps they'll come back.
Perhaps they'll stay faraway.
Leaving us with nothing but the dust
of who they used to be.

Margaret O. Daramola

You were gone
Long before you gathered the guts
To walk away
I saw it in your eyes each day
I felt it in the emptiness of your palms
You left.
Yet forced yourself to stay

Ghost Lovers

They will come,
awaken your love for them
awaken your desire
to make them your one and only,
awaken your expectation,
make you daydream,
make you believe
that you are their one and only.
Once your feelings reach the tip of a mountain,
once your euphoria meets its peak,
they will abandon you.
Walk away like they never knew you.
You will love them
but they will not love you.

Secrets

Sometimes I miss you.
Like really, deeply.
I miss you like earth misses rain in dry season.
I miss you like mother misses child when they are apart.
I miss you when solitude appears
in the shadow of the day.

But then it hails, and I am struck by lightning.
Which makes me remember
how cold and heartless you can be.
Which makes me wonder
if it is truly you I miss
or the person I thought you to be.
I think about you every night.
Every now and then I wonder if you do too.
Do you still remember me?
Or am I just another lost memory?

I forbid my thoughts from wandering in that direction,
but sometimes, I ask myself
if you've found someone else.
I mean, it has been a few moons already.
I think about you every day,
I feel so close to you.
But then again, I feel far away from you.

I don't know who you are.
And it scares me, that I am in love with a stranger.

Amertume

Il y a des jours où je pense à toi,
à ce que nous étions, à ce que nous aurions pu être.
Il y a des soirs où la mélancolie m'emporte,
des soirs où je suis perdue entre l'envie de te revoir
et le regret de t'avoir rencontré.

Margaret O. Daramola

Harm done in the name of love
is still harm and not love.

Again and again,
we talk about forgiving others
but no one ever told us
how hard it would be
to forgive ourselves.

Traces

He tells you that he will change
He begs for another chance
He promises to make things right

It's the first time

Yet something about his plea sounds so familiar
The way his voice quivers at every appeal
The anguish on his face
As teardrops dampen his smooth skin
It all takes you back to a well-known place

It's the first time

He claims
But it is *not* the first time for you.

It is said
that people learn to embrace the love
they think they are worthy of.
I should have known then
that I could never force my mother
to realize she deserved better.
I didn't know then
that I would one day have to force myself
to realize I deserve better.

Better

I always knew I deserved better
yet I never knew what better was.
I never knew how better should taste.
So I didn't know better
but to search for better
in all the wrong places.
I sought for a better in people
who only gave me worse.
I tainted their horns with angel rings.
I thought to myself that it was okay
to look past their flaws,
for the sake of having someone "better"
hold me tight and closer.

To belong. To uncover. To discover. To evolve. To love.
It's okay to love again, even if you've lost time
after time again.
It's okay to hope again, it's okay to try again.
'Again and again.

Burn the parts of you
that seek refuge in the pain,
the ones that secretly long for its return.
Use those ashes to write down testimonies.

Sometimes,
you'll have to cut people off.
Even if you don't want to.
Even if you love them.
Even if they love you.

Dancing With The Waves

Although your love made me drown,
I chose to share the beautiful memories instead.
The ones that made me want to swim in the first place.
Your eyes, took me on adventures
as unending as the ocean's seascape.
Your arms, gave me the same warmth
as water when it meets with earth.
And when I first met you,
I felt the same calm as the ocean on its peaceful days.

Although your *beauty* was what first attracted me,
I never knew how dangerous it would be
to swim alone in an ocean unknown.
No protection,
no knowledge of where these waves might take me.
I never knew how stormy it could get,
alone without a life jacket.
Unable to swim, to breathe or keep on floating.

But, although your love me drown,
I chose to share the beautiful things.
The ones that made me want to dive in the first place.

Because your love, my love, was the love that taught me
how to watch in troubled waters.
While I was trying to fight the waves, I realized the fight
was not mine, was never meant to be.

It was your love that taught me patience
when it feels as though you are sinking.
Faith, when all you see around you are angry waves.
Strength, when you've forgotten what it truly means.

Although your love made me drown,
I chose to write about the beautiful things instead.
The ones that made me want to swim in the first place.

Margaret O. Daramola

When the soil is dry and I have grown weary
Lord, teach me to always remember that you are there
with me.

Time Will Tell

You entered the train
invited by my gleam
charmed by my ray.
You took a seat beside mine.
Amazed. You wondered if this could all be real.
In ardor. You declared your love to me.

But you hadn't taken this train before
you didn't know it had a tendency
to move unexpectedly.
You didn't know that trains take you
through different lands in different times.

How would you cope
if the gleam that invited you
no longer attracted you?
If the glitter faded away
and these sparkles fell down like dead skin?

When you see the deepest parts of me
Will you still love me?
Will you still hold me?
Will you still ride on this train with me?

Silent Loss

When my lover found another way
I wrote the pain away.
When my best friend
walked away
I found no way
to externalize the turmoil I had within.
I allowed the rage to grow.
I invited the sadness to stay.
When my best friend walked away,
I couldn't *just* write the pain away.

Be patient with your wound.

Let it bleed.
Let it scar.
Let it heal.

Rocks

I remember walking
for what seemed to be an eternity
I remember hoping
that the weight would find another home to dwell in
I remember weeping
I remember screaming
I remember drowning
in a sorrow too deep to keep me floating
unable to see past my burden
I remember wondering
if ever I would feel light again
I remember hiding and isolating
thinking if I went unseen long enough
the heaviness wouldn't look for me
the fear wouldn't catch me
I remember aching
I remember praying
I remember hoping
I remember waiting and waiting and waiting

Cold Memories

I remember when freedom and I met
I was in the age of innocence.
We were close friends,
perhaps even best friends.
There were no barriers in my periphery,
or perhaps in my innocence
I was unaware of them.

I remember when freedom and I met
yet I don't remember the moment it left.
I can only reminisce the feeling it left me with.
Suddenly it was a stranger
and I became a foreigner in its midst.
Freedom
once felt so familiar.

Burning Rash

You lie on your bed
surrounded by walls
familiar to the drums
played by the thoughts in your head.
It isn't new to them,
these walls, know you better than that friend
who claims to ride with you and die with you.
They know you, they've seen the real you.
Every night, on your way back from a long day,
you meet them there,
ready to face the reality
you've been hiding from all day.

You try to go to sleep
but the lack of symphony, the lack of harmony
will keep you awake.
It will remind you of the bruises
you've failed to pay attention to.
It will remind you that they need care.
You will try to silence it
yet the drums will increase.

It is then, that you will know
that bruises avoided during the day
become thoughts that follow you through the night.
They do not disappear in the dark.

Margaret O. Daramola

You will beg for it to go
but it will stay–it will burn.
You will beg and beg and beg
it is then, that you will know
that bruises avoided during the day
become rash that burns throughout the night.

Intimacy

In the midnight hour
when the city has gone to sleep
but my eyelids refuse to do the same
I know that Adonai is still awake.
Therein I start a conversation with my Father.
I ask that He comes
to comfort the heart of his daughter.
I echo the ninety first Psalm of David.
My worship. My praise. I offer to my maker.
In the midnight hour,
I know He hears my prayer.

Today, I choose life.
These demons have been trying to convince me
otherwise.
But today, I choose life.
Tomorrow, when they come once more,
I will remember that if I have chosen life before,
I *can* and *shall* choose it again.

- You will not destroy me

You must wake up each morning
walk to your reflection
and
Remind yourself that you are worthy
even if you don't believe it
even if it breaks you to say it
Remind yourself that you are worthy

My Heart's Voice

If my heart could speak,
it would cry out–loud.
For all the nights it swallowed the truth
it was supposed to let out.
It would then whisper forgiveness
to all the other hearts
who did not know how to treat it right.
It would whisper forgiveness to itself
for all the bitterness
it allowed to stay in and rotten,
for allowing strangers to walk in
and misuse this heart,
my heart would forgive both I and them.
If my heart was gifted with lungs
it would sing lullabies to my unborn child.
Tell her it's okay
and pray that life treats her with love.
If my heart had lips
it would kiss the cheeks of the younger me,
tell her life gets better,
tell her to keep on breathing,
to keep on pushing, to keep on hoping.

This pain has something to teach you
you shouldn't force it away
nor should you allow it to overstay.

Daniel's Cry

I refuse to break bread

        until my prayers pass the third heaven
        until an Angel is sent back on my behalf

I refuse to break bread

        until these cells are open
        until these chains are broken

I will mourn
        until my grief is taken

Solitude

This night might find a way to scare you
with the thought
that you might not wake up
to see the light.
This journey might find a way to blind you
into believing
that it won't get any better,
into thinking that all is over.
I know it gets hard.
I know *hard* does not do justice to the difficulty.
I know you've been trying.
I know you've been pushing.
I know it feels like nobody knows
but I know you ain't tripping.
What you're feeling is real
and you have all the right
under the sun to feel that way.

Yet you must remember
never to give it more power than it already has.
Remember who you are.
Remember whose you are.
Don't over feed it,
don't allow it to overstay and please,
don't forget to send it away.

Margaret O. Daramola

Ties

She never enjoyed the ache,
she would long
for it to make its way out.
A close, yet unreliable friendship.
This type of pain
didn't get easier with time.
It hurt harder and harder each time.
The closer they got,
the more she bruised.
The more she bruised,
the more she ached.
She never got used to it.
She never loved it.
She never wanted it.

Although she hated her close friend
it seemed to love her.
It would leave
and come back unexpectedly.
And she, would invite it in,
preparing a feast to welcome it back.
Let it close,
creating a much stronger tie each time.

Perhaps in some way, she gave it permission to stay.
Perhaps if she really wanted to,
she could have sent it away.

I will not absorb the lies.
When they come in loud voices,
I will remember that the truth is even louder.

What do you do
and who do you turn to
when anxiety knocks on your door
for the third time in the same week
and you feel weak?
Do you lie on your bed,
cover your head
hoping the voices will go away?
Or do you stand on your feet and pray?
Do you accept it?
Or do you reject it?

Phobia

My body is the temple of the Lord,
Sacred and Holy.
At the front gate
you will find angels guarded at each corner
and when you enter,
you'll see a lobby decorated by truth.
On the ground, lays a carpet of faith.
There are towers of confidence standing tall
and the air you inhale overwhelms you with peace.

The only issue is
there are wounds in my heart
I haven't dealt with
I mean rooms in my temple
that are unreachable.
I've kept the keys hidden for so long,
I even buried some.
Day after day I neglect their existence
I forget
that there are rooms in this temple
that need to be rearranged.
I neglect and forget.
Until there's just a little bit of silence
or the wrong trigger
and that is how fear enters.

Takes hold of everything
you've tried so long to believe in.

Comes in and destroys the pillars of confidence
you've spent so much time building.

Fear. Never comes alone.
It comes with memories and voices.
Fear. Never walks alone.
Sometimes it knocks,
other times it meets the doors open
and invites itself into your temple.
Blurring the windows of your mind with lies
dusting your carpet of faith with doubt.

Armless. Is how I feel whenever you come in.
A dangerous type of vulnerability
I open up the doors to you
as if I do not know you came to haunt me.
Powerless. Is the atmosphere whenever you are near.

Fear. Never comes alone.
It comes with memories and voices.
Fear. Never walks alone.
Its footsteps follow uncertainty and anxiety.

When your mind
mistakes what could be for reality.
When your body
starts to cripple and feels disable.
When you are drowning in cold sweat.
When the past
tries to come back to life.

Invite the Spirit!
Tell it who your God is!
Tell it that if God has not given you the spirit of fear
then fear has nothing to do in your temple.
Open those hidden rooms,
let Him heal those unsealed wounds.
Sweep away the dust left by doubt,
let your ground shine in faith again.
Clean the lies left on your window
let your lobby regain truth.

Because remember,
Your body is the temple of the Lord,
Sacred and Holy.

Margaret O. Daramola

Better days are coming.

II

I want to go blind for you, Lord.
Teach me
not to walk in the direction
that I have set for myself,
but to rejoice in the path
that you have set for me.
On days
when I feel caged and I feel blocked,
teach me to see myself
the way that you see me.

The bleeding is not eternal
if my skin can scar
then my heart can too.

Margaret O. Daramola

Home Ticket

When will you come back to yourself?
You've been on a voyage trying to be somebody else
for far too long, honey.
Don't overstay your welcome in a stranger's body
come back home–where you truly belong.

Old Petals

I once held fear in the depth of my core.
I sat in fear,
afraid of the power people may have over me,
afraid of the pain it might cause me,
afraid of suffering the anguish
of another broken heart.
Afraid.
I soon realized that
it was not pain that I feared the most,
it was the thought
of not healing from another wound
that made me cringe.

Behind my fear of pain,
was actually lack of faith in God.
Because if God
truly is as great as I claim Him to be,
then no amount of pain could ever destroy me.
No heartache is greater than His power or His love.
I learned to believe that God will catch me if I fall.
I learned to believe that the *hurting power* within humans
is nowhere near the healing power within God.

New Petals

I had to learn to forgive.

Not only the people who cut me open–causing my blood
to leak. But also, and mostly, myself. No one hurt me
more than I hurt myself. No one told me to go back to the
very things that destroyed me. Yet, there I was. No one
asked me to find refuge in the very thing that left me
empty. Yet, I made it my home–decorating it to my
liking and still, I watched it drain me.

Yes. I owe myself the biggest apology.

But lately, I've been learning, learning to unlearn.
Lately, I've been blooming–differently.
I've been discovering a new me.
I've been divorcing, burning and uprooting the old me.

Fresh Seeds

I took the hate,
the bitterness and the regret.
I buried them all.
But somehow
they seem to have found their way
back into my heart.
Perhaps they were still alive at their funeral.

In this new season
in order to bloom persistently,
I must dig deep into my heart
and uproot the seeds of bitterness planted therein.

So next season
Hatred and Regret will not find space to resurrect.

This. is the pain
I tried so hard to avoid while I was still with you.
This. is the pain
I was so afraid of.
This. is the pain
I thought was strong enough to end me.
This. is the pain
I am currently surviving.
This. is the pain
That is turning me into a heroine.

When it's been over a year
and melancholy tries to find its way
back into your heart.
Remember this time,
that the choice is *yours*
to give it the keys or to keep them to yourself,
to unplug old scars or to keep them sealed.

You have the authority to step on the rocks that try to keep you captive.

Lessons

I used to wonder
how people's hearts suddenly turned so cold.
How they would *love* you on Saturday
but *neglect* you on Monday,
purposely leaving a day in between
for you to soak in hope,
only to dry it out with doubt.
Until I understood that
a cold heart is nothing but a bleeding heart.
Unlike skin that burns when it is cut
the human heart freezes when it is wounded.
The only fire it needs to heal is Love.

Moonlight

I watch the moon and she inspires me.
I wonder if up there she ever gets lonely,
if she is ever jealous of the sun or
if on the contrary
she embraces the light that through her shines
in the absence of company.

The moon reminds me of me.
The way she curves on some nights
and is whole on other nights.
Her mystery. Her gleam. Her beauty.

Perhaps in reality
the moon never gets lonely.
Perhaps she carries secrets that keep her company.
Perhaps in reality
the sun is the one that envies her mystery.

Snail

It rains outside
It rains heavier on the inside
It's dark outside
And the lights have gone missing
For way too long on the inside
I sit
I notice a snail appear while no one is watching

It crawls.   I feel a pinch in the cage of my left rib.

It stops.   I am caught unable to exhale.

It hides sometimes.   I pause.

As I sit, watching this snail crawl on empty streets,
I think of names to give it.
Perhaps I should call it healing,
Because it comes out after the rain,
It crawls, it stops,
It even hides sometimes.
But never for too long,
When the sun rises, it'll be there
For everyone to see.

Familiar

He came to my door
with all the gifts I had been praying for.
Yet I found myself locked on the inside
unable to open the door.

On the inside I was unsure
if this truly were the gifts
I had been waiting for.

I had seen something similar before.
Gifts wrapped in the most colorful of ribbons,
packed with care and attention.
So without hesitation,
I had rushed to open my door.

Yet when those ribbons had fallen off,
when my eyes had opened up
to what it was that I had welcomed into my first floor.
I quickly lost my awe
and it was there that I learned to close my door.
It was there that I learned to stay indoor.

Yet for years I found myself closing my door,
unable to open up
to the very gifts I had been praying for.

Unfamiliar

How can I love you?
Winter feels more familiar
Than the warmth you bring.

*Do not allow the disappointments of yesterday
to hinder you from receiving the blessings of today.*

A Letter To My Future Lover

Dear future lover,
I'm sorry if I'm too cold at times,
life hasn't been very soft with me.
Sometimes, it's hard to remember how to be gentle.
But believe me, I am trying.
I'm sorry if I don't open up
when you ask me what's wrong.
Please love, don't take it personally.
For some people, it just isn't that easy.
Forgive me in advance,
if you ever catch me doubting
the truth beneath your words.
How do I explain that
life hasn't treated us all equally.

Dear future lover,
I promise to love you fearlessly.
I promise to love you freely
in spite of the weight life once put on me.
Despite the cicatrix even you cannot see.
Baby, I promise not to make you pay
for the sins of another.

Searching for healing in another person
will not grant you the closure you are looking for.

Unequipped

When the vase fell to the ground
you suddenly forgot about its beauty.
It was no longer the aesthetics that attracted you
but a sense of pity.
A pity that drew you *too* close.

You think you are a savior.

You think it is your duty
to fix what's broken.
But remember–shattered pieces will cut anyone
who tries to come near
whether they come with good intentions or not.
Shattered vases will cut you if you come unequipped.

- *Not Your Battle*

Self-Love

In a garden of roses, you are a human sunflower.
Self-love means recognizing that sometimes you may be
the one with unhealthy petals. Self-love means allowing
the Gardener to cut those petals off, even if it hurts you
in the process. Self-love, my dear, means staying away
from whatever keeps your petals from blooming as
colorfully as they should.

Dawn Light

I remember instinctively
keeping my eyes fixed on the horizon.
Because the horizon
spoke to me in a hopeful language.
A language quite different
than the one I had become so familiar with.
So I kept my eyes fixed on the horizon,
in hopes of one day becoming fluent in its language.

And suddenly, the ache was no more.

Dazzle

Peafowl

Even if you place me in a cage,
my wings will spread.
For I am as a peafowl,
too persistent to be tamed.
I was born to fly.
These bars
cannot take purpose away from me.
I will always break free.
I will always break loose.
I will go beyond anything
that tries to repress me.
There truly is something powerful
within my feathers.
Because even if you place me in a cage
my wings will spread.

Summer Solstice

When your trauma is over,
you stand in disbelief of your survival.
You forget the freezing air
that once stopped you from breathing.
You don't know when the Winter ended,
you don't remember seeing the Spring coming.
But suddenly, it is Summer.
And you are no longer paralyzed.

You take a walk outside,
see flowers have taken a bright color,
one you do not remember seeing before.
Last time you checked,
they were all grey and petalless.
You wonder if it is all true.

There you are, breathing again.
Clap for yourself honey.
You survived.

The Taste of Healing

I feel healed,
I no longer have blood
leaking to the ground.
I've put on plasters
and mopped the floor
way too many times.
So I know,
because I no longer see red dots
on the ground.
My tears,
no longer force their way out of my eyes.

I am no longer drained.

My muscles
no longer feel the heaviness
of constantly being drawn towards gravity.
My thoughts
no longer leave for unhealthy journeys.
They've found track in what is true and right.

I have regained strength.

It's like I see clearer now.
Yet I still remember how it feels
to watch myself drowning
in an ocean of melancholy.

To see something as beautiful as life
and look at it disgustingly.
I still remember how it feels
to look at myself
and see nothing but shattered pieces.

I feel healed,
I see agony as nothing but a faraway memory.

Bareness

I planted sunflowers on dry soil.
I then wondered why I saw no harvest,
I wondered what I could possibly have done wrong.
A season of aching, breaking and weeping.

In the midst of my barren crops, I quickly realized
that certain seeds are too precious to be planted just
anywhere, some seeds need special care.

Above all I am grateful for my season of loss and
mourning. How would I have known otherwise that
nothing was wrong with my seeds in the first place?

If it hadn't been for my barrenness,
I'd still be lost, planting sunflowers on dry soil.

We Live

How many of us
have gone to sleep
wearing sadness on our chests?
Mourning the death
of a loved one,
a friend,
or even ourselves?
We.
The ones who
should have been broken.
The ones who
could have dried out in the drought.
We.
Are instead the ones
who still sing lullabies.
We still whisper to the wind
when it passes by.
We still find means to live.
Again, again and again.
We live.

The Aftermath

A few moons have gone by now
and I am at that stage
where I put on my garment
and praise the Almighty.

I look in the mirror
and see a masterpiece.
I didn't know it would look this beautiful
during the making.
When I saw those pencils drop
and those colors burst,
I thought the oeuvre
would be ruined.
I couldn't see the beauty
in the painting.

But a year has gone by now
and I am at that stage
where I have learned
not to cringe
at the sight of a messy painting
but to smile
at the masterpiece in the making.

"Stranger"

Allow me to see
The parts of you that hide 'neath
The soil of your past

Leave fear behind–come
Free as a dove in the sky
I will not judge you

I want to know you
For you, beyond the aged clay
That covers your heart.

If I Ever Forget

If I ever forget the strength that I carry
Remind me
that I was born a warrior.
Remind me
of the weapons of survival stored in my veins.
Remind me
that I know what it means to fight.
To actually fight.
Fight to win
when your body has given up on you.
Fight to stay alive
when depression keeps trying to kill you.
Fight to keep you near.
Fight to keep you here.
Fight.
If ever I fall short and forget.
Please,
dare to remind me.

Gentle Reminders

And whenever your past
tries to start a conversation with you

Remind her
to stay away from you.

Remind her
that you are someone new.

Remind her
that the dead and the living
are of two different worlds.

Foreign Taste

That day,
it was poison that walked in.
I embraced it,
took it in and allowed it to overstay.
It couldn't end me,
yet it left its bitter taste behind.

The following day,
when medicine came close,
it had such a foreign taste,
that I didn't know how to take it in.

Medicine,
tasted nothing like the poison I was used to.
And although it was good for me,
I struggled severely to let it in.

Unlearning trauma,
it is painful
it is exhausting
it is draining.

But above all,
it is necessary.

Q&A

Q: How do you know when you've moved on?

A: I don't think there comes a time where it becomes unknown to you. Yet I do believe there comes one where the memory no longer haunts you. It will no longer hold the same power over you, nor will it find the means to control you. You might never fully forget, but you will learn to let go, and you will grow.

Q: So what do I do while I wait?

A: But darling, you do not wait.
You seek healing. You seek counseling.
You seek God, through prayer and fasting.

I learned the hard way
that you do not have to suffer
for true love to come your way.

When you find something as rare and beautiful as a treasure, when you find someone worth taking along on your journey, make sure you let go of the heavy, unnecessary baggage you carry. In order to embrace the fullness of the treasure you see.

Treasure

You are like a treasure to me.
Hard to find,
grateful when you do.
I've been searching for you
all my life.
And now that I finally have you
here
by my side,
I struggle to believe that it is you.
I struggle to believe that you are real.
I struggle with the thought of you being
here
by my side.
I've been knocking on deaf doors,
searching empty cities,
I've been hoping,
hoping and failing.
I've given up and I've let go.
But you are like a treasure to me.
The type you find
when you least expect it.
The type that comes
when you've totally given up on it.

Dove

When we sought God, when we asked Him to come, when we opened the door and allowed Him in, when we washed our masks, when we humbled ourselves, destroying the walls we had created–to keep us from loving, hoping, aching and breaking. When we showed Him the truest parts of ourselves, He began to feel comfortable in the rooms we had on lock. He began to clean them up–taking out the dirt that covered us with shame. He arranged our broken vases and reframed our self-portrays. He began to own our homes, we began to feel clean, we began to feel pure. Once we allowed Him in, we began to heal.

Old Belongings

When beauty
is a foreign concept to you.
When shackles
are the closest you've ever been to jewelry.
When you've learned
to wear them with a smile.
You've learned
to carry this weight without a limp.
You've learned
to embrace all that held you down.

Then suddenly,
You learn
that you could be free.
You learn
about the possibility
of walking as softly as the wind,
without ever being tied to that heavy jewelry.
You find out that this weight you thought was yours
was never really yours to carry.
Yes, you've learned that you *could* be free.
Yet what you haven't learned yet
is how to let go of old belongings.

Dear Father

As you are seated
on your heavenly throne
pouring down your love to your children.
Please,
teach me to recognize in Christ
the love that you have for me.
Teach me to accept it
when it comes my way.
After I've grown comfortable
in the midst of shackles
and freedom feels like winter
in a foreign country,
teach me to accept the gifts that you have for me.
When they come
knocking on my door,
teach me to make room for them.
Teach me to invite them in.
Teach me to welcome them home.

This, I pray in the name of the one,
whose example of love I long to follow,
your Son, Jesus Christ.

These Days

It still triggers me
but it no longer
controls me.
When it tries to come in,
I know now,
how to keep my doors shut.
When I hear those footsteps from afar,
I know not to let it in.
I know how to recognize it
for what it truly is,
even when it knocks on my weakest door.

I know you.
I see you.
This phobia,
has never been the type to come alone.
It is known to walk together
with memories and voices,
to find refuge in old wounds.

There was a time where I knew not
how to chase it away.
I thought, I just had to embrace it.
I thought, I just had to live with it.
But now,
I recognize it for what it truly is.
I know how to send it away.

Yet sometimes,
it still triggers me.
But you will find me rejoicing,
for it no longer has the power
to control me.

Growth

They don't tell you what it takes to get here. When they tell you to go, they fail to mention the hurdles that will come to keep you company. For so long they will be present; you will forget what it feels like to be free. You will forget yourself. Forget who you used to be. There. Alone. You will forget your identity. For so long it will burn. But it will not be the end of you. There. Alone. You will learn to fly again, you will trust the power in your wings. You will learn that these hurdles cannot keep you captive unless you allow them to. In your solitude, you will learn to be free–again.

Ashes

Burning bridges with the woman
that I used to be.
With the insecurities that held me down
and held me bound.
With the lies tatted on my mind.
I'm lighting a fire on the doors I left opened,
allowing fear, sadness and torment into my life.
I'm taking authority.
And I'm leaving these ashes behind me.

No one ever goes through the fire
and comes out the same.

Strongholds

When will you realize
that your battles
have been against the same foe
wearing different garments each time?
If truly you want to win,
you must find out who the secret man is
that hides behind those misleading costumes.

Wanderer

He came back home.
When we crossed each other's paths,
it was no longer a stranger that I saw
in the sparkle of his brown eyes.
He came back home
from a long and stormy journey.
I wonder if he'll ever tell me
the lessons he learned
while he was away.
I wonder how life treated him
while he was long gone.
But he came back home.
I instantly recognized him in the crowd.
I used to see him regularly
without ever truly seeing him
so when I finally saw him again
I knew he was back home–to himself.

We all bleed the same
behind our tittles, degrees, and classes,
behind everything created to separate us.
We all bleed the same color.
No matter the severity of our wound
or the area in which we were cut.
We all *bleed* the same.

A.Z.

Your name embodies freedom
but sometimes you feel caged.
And it's okay.
It's okay to shrink.
It's okay to sink
with both arms begging for revival.
But it is not okay
to forget that your name means freedom.
The same resurrection power
that raised The Messiah,
is the same one tatted in your veins.
By that same Name you are revived.
Always remember who you are
even when your feelings fail to convince you.

Grudges

You claim to have forgiven
but your heart still aches
at the sight of that person.
Your bones still quiver
at the thought of that person.
Then perhaps, in reality
you haven't truly forgiven.

You must learn
that there is but a thin line
between guarding your heart
and blocking your blessing.

Imagine the person you would be
if you actually took the time to heal.

Captives

Slaves, in another man's land.
Working and sweating
under foreign weather.
They cried out to The Most High.

For 400 years, they were captives.
Chained, in bondage mentally and physically.
They cried out to The Most High.
Pleading for His mercy,
begging to be free.

He, in His sovereignty,
showed them His mercy.
He sent Moses,
He parted the red sea so they could be free.
He sent Harriet, He delivered you from slavery.

With the joy of a dove,
they glanced around in freedom,
they quickly forgot about the God
who had set them free.
They went back to astrology,
went back to sorcery.
Bowing their heads to gods made of wood,
silver and gold,
they worshipped the dead.

They defiled themselves.

They defiled the temple
that was created to give Him glory.
They turned their backs and turned their hearts.
They caused the King of Kings
to be grieved in His heart.
And He warned them saying,

"If my people
who are called by my name
will humble themselves and pray
and seek my face
and turn from their wicked ways,
I will hear from heaven
and I will forgive their sins and restore their land."

Yet they mocked His voice.
They Neglected His warnings.
And ended up trapped in exile,
captive a second time.

What if they had obeyed Him?
Honoring his very first commandment that says,
"Thou shall have no other gods before me!"

What if. What if. What if.

What if you can't see the God that freed you
Because you look at Him
Through the lens of the one that held you captive.

Surrender

Allow Him to be your leader.
You will lose sleep
trying to find your way
without a Shepherd.
You will exhaust yourself
trying to save yourself.

Surrender

And remember that Christ,
on Calvary already took the victory.

Margaret O. Daramola

Up-root

Like Saul
I must lose sight
Of the logic within my path
Until I am made to Paul

Reborn

A lamb after true Light

In the sky, where I never thought I'd be.
All this liberty is new to me
Lord, I never knew I could be this free.

- To God be the Glory

III

Victory

I have memories of that day as if it were yesterday.
The day two wings placed me on a path I knew nothing
about. Their wings–so light yet so heavy, so bright that
their gleam overwhelmed my sight. It was like a dream to
me. I remember as they graciously led me towards my
first steps, the ease I felt, the confidence I had. Although
this path was foreign to me, I trusted the wings who had
placed me there.

Now, it didn't take long until I began to thirst.
My mouth ran dry and my thoughts began to wander in
search for water. At that moment, it felt as though every
water fountain had run dry, yet it was in the bareness of
that season, that I set my eyes on an overflowing
fountain. I felt beyond refreshed, watching my steps
regain their pace with blissful ease. Satisfaction in my
tongue, I quickly forgot about how far I'd come.

As I found myself walking through my journey,
I began to hunger. A hunger that profoundly cut me.
Unlike my thirst, this hunger made me wonder if ever I
will be filled again. Emptiness soon became my closest
companion. I had gotten so used to the taste of bitterness,
that I allowed it to overstay. But it was when I least
expected it, when I thought I'd never see it, that my
hunger escaped for a faraway country. Although it left
me physically, it failed to vanish spiritually. I now had
PTSD of what it feels like to be hungry.

I walked. Continuing my journey on this path. It seemed safe and quiet on most days. I felt free, furthering my steps without worry. Until I began to feel under my feet the sensation of a rock. It did not hurt much at first, nor did it cause me any harm. The real trouble appeared when these rocks came consistently. Each step I took would be a reminder of the severe pain it may cause me. And slowly, I ceased to walk.

The idea of moving forward only brought with it fear and anxiety. I slurred the wings who had placed me on this path, why had they left me here alone with bleeding feet? How was I supposed to express gratitude towards a great God when it seemed as though each time I'd call upon His name, bigger rocks would come my way?

Exhausted and mentally drained, I lost complete confidence in the wings who had placed me on this unknown path. Where did my ease go to? Where in this journey did I allow my excitement to expire? These rocks made my feet damp in blood. I no longer desired to further my steps. I stopped. Accepted misfortune as my fate, I ceased to believe that anything good would come out of this path. I slowly began to lose my strength, my focus, I slowly began to doubt if perhaps the light that I had seen at the very beginning of my path was not a simple illusion.

I was lost in despair, because there I was in the middle of nowhere, waiting and hoping for someone to see me.

It seemed as though the angels who had placed me on this very path had forgotten all about me. I allowed a rock to make a home of my pathway. I allowed it to block my sight and stop me from moving. I allowed a rock to distort my vision. All I saw was a stumbling block.

And when I thought I couldn't fall any further than this, I heard a voice say to me, "Why are you doubting me? I quenched your thirst, I fed you when you were hungry, I placed you on this path for my glory. Now, take the authority I have given to you and speak to the rock you see in front you!"
I still remember the ease I felt, the confidence I had, although this path was foreign to me, I recognized the voice speaking to me. So soft, yet so demanding. I then go ahead; I speak to these rocks that had provoked my bleeding. I speak to the rock that had made stagnant for so long. I speak to my early ages of PTSD caused by an unending hunger inside of me. I speak authoritatively to all these obstacles, obeying the command of His voice.

And as I walk away from a stone that had kept me captive for so long, I begin to see a light so bright, one similar to the gleam carried by the two wings who had placed me on this very path. This light caused me to fall face down on my knees and praise He who had placed me here. This path was never designed to destroy me. This path was for me to be able to share with you a testimony. This path was for you, too, to see the beauty in your journey.

126

And now that I see the light, I stand in disbelief
as to how I ever allowed little rocks to keep me from
walking. How did I allow these obstacles to lead me into
such deception? He had been with me all along. The one
I failed to see while I was focused on the wrong.

About the Author

Margaret Daramola is a Nigerian born writer, spoken word artist and public speaker. Raised in Switzerland, she began writing at an early age. Her High School thesis consisted of a collection of poems entitled *Slam Poetry on Human Rights and Injustice*, which led her to speaking engagements at major conferences and events organized by the African Union, the Swiss Agency for Development and Cooperation and Women's Hope International among several others. She currently studies Creative Writing and History at Hampton University in Virginia, where she simultaneously serves as a Christian ministry leader and an NCAA Division 1 Athlete.

Keep in touch with Margaret Daramola for news on her next book and many other exclusives.

Website: www.maggiedaramola.com
Instagram: @Maggie.Daramola

Made in the USA
Middletown, DE
09 October 2023